THE GREAT BIBLE DISCOVERY

PHARISEES, SADDUCEES AND ESSENES

THE BIBLE IS A BEST-SELLER. IT IS ALSO ONE OF THE MASTER-WORKS OF WORLD LITERATURE - SO IMPORTANT THAT UNIVERSITIES TODAY TEACH 'NON-RELIGIOUS' BIBLE COURSES TO HELP STUDENTS WHO CHOOSE TO STUDY WESTERN LITERATURE.

THE BIBLE POSSESSES AN AMAZING POWER TO FASCINATE YOUNG AND OLD ALIKE.

ONE REASON FOR THIS UNIVERSAL APPEAL IS THAT IT DEALS WITH BASIC HUMAN LONGINGS, EMOTIONS, RELATIONSHIPS. 'ALL THE WORLD IS HERE.' ANOTHER REASON IS THAT SO MUCH OF THE BIBLE CONSISTS OF STORIES. THEY ARE FULL OF MEANING BUT EASY TO REMEMBER.

HERE ARE THOSE STORIES, PRESENTED SIMPLY AND WITH A MINIMUM OF EXPLANATION. WE HAVE LEFT THE TEXT TO SPEAK FOR ITSELF. GIFTED ARTISTS USE THE ACTION-STRIP TECHNIQUE TO BRING THE BIBLE'S DEEP MESSAGE TO READERS OF ALL AGES. THEIR DRAWINGS ARE BASED ON INFORMATION FROM ARCHAEOLOGICAL DISCOVERIES COVERING FIFTEEN CENTURIES.

AN ANCIENT BOOK - PRESENTED FOR THE PEOPLE OF THE SECOND MILLENNIUM. A RELIGIOUS BOOK - PRESENTED FREE FROM THE INTERPRETATION OF ANY PARTICULAR CHURCH. A UNIVERSAL BOOK - PRESENTED IN A FORM THAT ALL MAY ENJOY.

M publishing
CARLISLE, UK

18

The Greek translation of the Old Testament contained some books which were not included in the Hebrew original, which was read in the synagogues. These books are called deutero-canonical by Roman Catholics and Orthodox Christians, who regard them as inspired. Other branches of the Christian church refer to them as the Apocrypha and do not think of them as Scripture. The Church of England says they contain helpful guidance for life but are not to be used to define what Christians should believe.

These books vary greatly. Some are short novels, such as Judith and Tobias and the Angel, some historical accounts like 1 & 2 Maccabees. One of them, known as the Book of Wisdom, is a very skilful attempt to present an Old Testament view of God and the world in a way which Greeks would understand and value.

Some Jews would have thought highly of such a book, written (probably) by a Greek-speaking Jew of Alexandria who wanted to find common ground between Greek culture and Judaism. Others would have disapproved of trying to do this.

The Essenes, for example, were a group which rejected any form of compromise and detested Greek culture. They were shocked at the way in which John Hyrcanus, son of Simon Maccabeus, the first of the Hasmonean rulers, combined military and priestly functions. The Essenes formed communities in remote places, such as Qumran where the so-called Dead Sea scrolls were found. There they worshipped and kept the law of Moses in the hope that by doing so they might hasten the coming of the messiah.

The Sadducees had no problem with accepting worldly power. For many years they worked closely with the Hasmoneans, accepting their claim to high-priestly authority and gaining great influence over everything to do with the Temple.

Like the Essenes, the Pharisees were opposed to Greek culture. Many of their party fought alongside the Maccabees. But they were not happy about the Hasmonean claim to the office of high priest. Also they were greatly concerned with ceremonial purity, which was difficult to preserve if one tried to mix secular affairs with Temple rituals. One of the Hasmonean rulers even crucified 800 Pharisees. His widow, however, favoured them, and made sure they were well represented in the Sanhedrin or Jewish council.

The conflict between Pharisees and Sadducees surfaces here and there in the New Testament. The Essenes are there too, but only in the background.

TOBIT

JUDITH

ECCLESIASTICUS

THE BOOK OF WISDOM (WISDOM OF SOLOMON)

PHARISEES, SADDUCEES AND ESSENES

First published as *Découvrir la Bible* 1983

First edition © Larousse S.A. 1984
24-volume series adaptation by Mike Jacklin © Knowledge Unlimited 1994
This edition © OM Publishing 1995

01 00 99 98 97 96 95   7 6 5 4 3 2 1

OM Publishing is an imprint of Send the Light Ltd.,
P.O. Box 300, Carlisle, Cumbria CA3 0QS, U.K.

Introductions: Peter Cousins

British Library Cataloguing in Publication Data
A catalogue record for this book is available from the British Library
ISBN 1-85078-222-9

Printed in Singapore by Tien Wah Press (Pte) Ltd.

TOBIT

THIS IS THE STORY OF TOBIT, OF THE TRIBE OF NAPHTALI, WHO WAS DEPORTED TO NINEVEH, AND OF HIS SON, TOBIAS.

SCENARIO: Etienne DAHLER
DRAWING: Raymond POÏVET

LIGHT SHINES ON THE GOOD PEOPLE

HERE I AM, POOR AND BLIND! BUT GOD KNOWS I'VE LIVED A GOOD LIFE. EVERYBODY SPOKE WELL OF ME. KINGS TRUSTED THE ADVICE I GAVE THEM...

TOBIAS LOOKED FOR SOMEONE TO GUIDE HIM ON SUCH A LONG JOURNEY.

WHO ARE YOU?

AZARIAS, AN ISRAELITE. I KNOW ALL THE ROADS OF MEDIA.

AZARIAS WAS INTRODUCED TO TOBIT.

I'M A LIVING CORPSE!

GOD WILL CURE YOU.

TOBIT, WHY ARE YOU SENDING OUR SON TO GET THIS MONEY?

ANNA, THERE'S ANOTHER REASON FOR THIS JOURNEY...

...AND TOBIAS AND HIS COMPANION SET OFF FOR ECBATANA.

TOBIAS, THIS IS A GOOD PLACE TO SPEND THE NIGHT.

AT THE EDGE OF THE LAKE...

I'VE CAUGHT A BIG ONE! IT'S HURTING ME!

DON'T LET IT GO!

...TOBIAS STARTED TO FISH.

THIS IS AN UNUSUAL KIND OF FISH. THE HEART AND LIVER DRIVE AWAY DEMONS, AND THE GALL CURES BLINDNESS.

TOMORROW WE'LL BE WITH YOUR COUSIN SARAH. SHE'LL BECOME YOUR WIFE, ACCORDING TO THE LAW OF MOSES.

BUT, AZARIAS, ALL HER HUSBANDS DIE!

TOBIAS, REMEMBER THE FISH'S HEART AND LIVER...

7

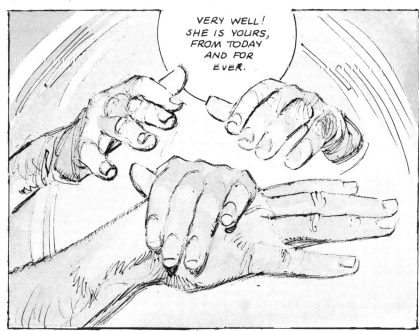

A FEW DAYS LATER AZARIAS RETURNED WITH GABAEL.

TOBIAS, YOU'RE THE IMAGE OF YOUR FATHER! HERE IS THE MONEY AND MY PRESENTS!

AFTER THE WEDDING-FEAST RAGUEL SAID GOOD-BYE...

TOBIAS, TAKE HALF OF ALL I HAVE; YOU'LL GET THE REST WHEN I DIE.

TOBIAS, WE'RE GETTING NEAR TO NINEVEH. LET THE TWO OF US GO ON AHEAD, TO FIND YOUR PARENTS.

TOBIT! THEY'RE COMING!

TOBIAS, DON'T FORGET THE FISH-GALL.

TOBIAS PUT THE GALL ON HIS FATHER'S EYES, AND SUDDENLY...

I CAN SEE! MY SON! LIGHT OF MY LIFE!

TOBIAS, PAY AZARIAS HIS WAGES. HE DESERVES A BIG BONUS.

I AM RAPHAEL, ONE OF THE SEVEN ANGELS WHO STAND IN GOD'S PRESENCE. HAPPY ARE THOSE TO WHOM HE SENDS ME!

WHEN YOU WERE IN TROUBLE, TOBIT, IT WAS I WHO CARRIED YOUR PRAYERS TO GOD. HE SAW HOW YOU HELPED THE POOR. THE PRAYERS OF GOOD PEOPLE ARE ALWAYS ANSWERED.

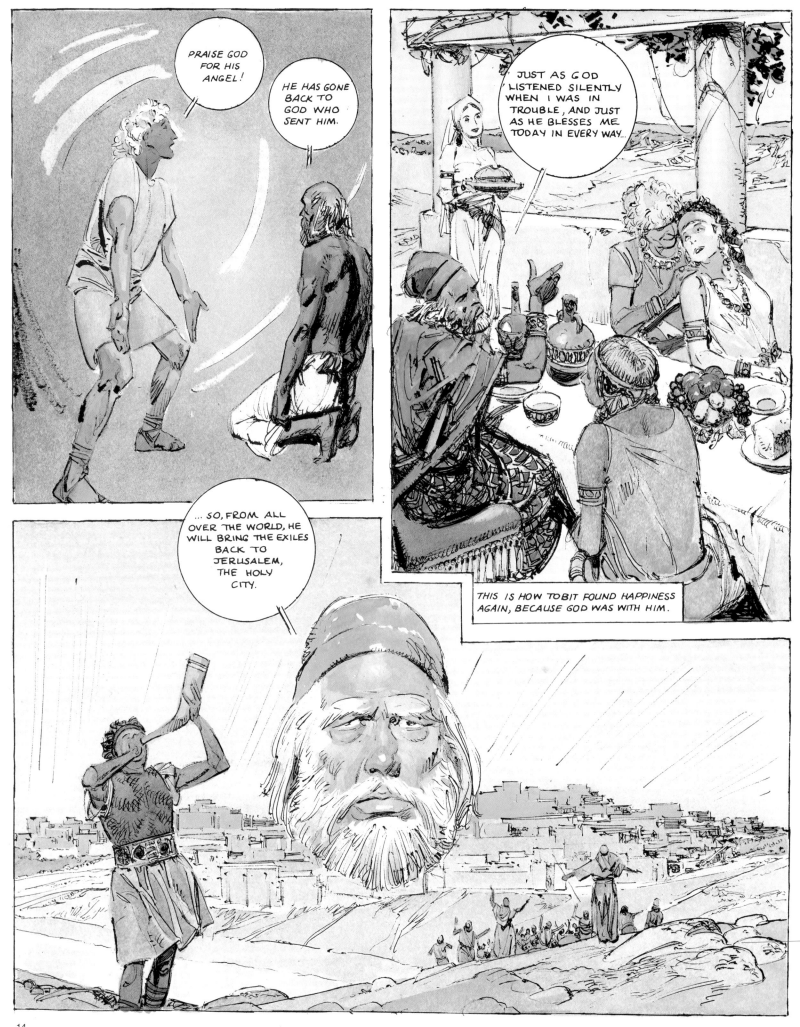

JUDITH
the heroine of Bethulia

And Achior was taken near to **Bethulia**, a town which was holding out against Holophernes.

They took Achior to **Ozias**, the magistrate of Bethulia.

VERY SOON THE ARMY OF HOLOPHERNES WAS CAMPED OUTSIDE THE WALLS OF BETHULIA...

THIS TOWN GETS ITS WATER FROM SPRINGS AT THE FOOT OF THE HILL... WE'LL STOP THE PEOPLE FROM LEAVING THE TOWN... THEN THIRST WILL FORCE THEM TO SURRENDER.

NOBODY CAN CAPTURE THAT TOWN, BUT THEY'LL HAVE TO GIVE IN SOON.

AS THE DAYS WENT BY...

MOTHER, I'M THIRSTY!

OZIAS, THIS IS YOUR FAULT! WE SHOULD HAVE SURRENDERED!

BROTHERS, LET US GIVE THE LORD FIVE MORE DAYS TO SAVE US, THEN WE'LL GIVE OURSELVES UP.

24

25

UNDER ROME'S YOKE

JOHN HYRCANUS SUCCEEDED HIS FATHER, SIMON MACCABAEUS. HE WAS PROCLAIMED HIGH PRIEST AND GOVERNOR IN JERUSALEM.

HYRCANUS, MANY OF THE **CHASÎDÎM***, AND ESPECIALLY THE MOST RELIGIOUS OF THEM, DON'T LIKE YOU. YOU SHOULD NOT TRUST THEM.

*Members of a religious party which had supported the Maccabees.

SCENARIO: Etienne DAHLER
DRAWING: José BIELSA

IN FACT...

THAT IS CORRECT. IF HE IS TO HOLD THAT OFFICE, A MAN MUST DESCEND FROM THE HIGH PRIEST **ZADOK**.

BUT I SEEM TO THINK THERE IS A GROUP WHICH SUPPORTS ME...

WE MUST SUPPORT HYRCANUS, AND MAKE HIM STRONGER.

LATER ON WE'LL HAVE A HIGH PRIEST IN KEEPING WITH THE TRADITION.

AND HYRCANUS DOESN'T!

THEN HE IS A FRAUD!

THAT IS TRUE; THE **SADDUCEES** ARE ON YOUR SIDE.

FOR THE MOMENT THE IMPORTANT THING IS TO BE FREE, SO WE CAN LIVE BY THE LAW OF MOSES.

A LITTLE LATER THE ARMY OF ANTIOCHUS BROKE CAMP...

WHAT BAD LUCK! OUR CITY IS NOTHING BUT RUINS!

NOT THE FIRST TIME, EITHER! BUT WE'LL REBUILD THE FORTIFICATIONS... AND THAT WILL BE JUST THE START...

JERUSALEM IS BANDAGING HER WOUNDS...

IT WOULD HAVE BEEN BETTER IF SHE HADN'T BEEN WOUNDED AT ALL!

CHASÎD, WHAT DO YOU MEAN?

AS LONG AS ISRAEL IS UNFAITHFUL TO THE LORD, SHE'LL HAVE BAD LUCK...

HYRCANUS ISN'T DESCENDED FROM DAVID OR ZADOK! HE SHOULDN'T BE THE KING OR THE HIGH PRIEST. HE IS MEDDLING IN PAGAN POLITICS... AND WE'RE PAYING THE PRICE.

THE CHASIDIM WERE CLOSE TO THE PEOPLE, AND URGED THEM TO REBEL...

WITH SUCH A KING WE'LL NEVER BE ABLE TO LIVE IN PEACE!

HE IS RIGHT! LET US GET RID OF THIS IMPOSTOR!

HYRCANUS MUST DIE!

THE PEOPLE REVOLTED, BUT HYRCANUS HARSHLY CRUSHED THE REBELLION.

I'VE WARNED THEM! IN TIME THEY'LL LEARN THAT I WANT TO BE THEIR LEADER!

HYRCANUS IS STILL VERY STRONG. IT IS A MISTAKE TO ATTACK HIM HEAD-ON.

I THINK WE MUST LIVE ACCORDING TO THE LAW OF MOSES, INSTEAD OF GETTING MIXED UP IN POLITICAL STRUGGLES.

WHAT DO YOU MEAN?

THEN ALL THE RELIGIOUS LEADERS GOT TOGETHER - EXCEPT THE SADDUCEES.

THE WHOLE WORLD DOES WHAT IS WRONG. AND GOOD NEVER COMES FROM WRONG! WE'RE GOD'S PEOPLE, THE CHILDREN OF LIGHT! LET US LIVE APART FROM THE WORLD, SO WE CAN KEEP THE COMMANDMENTS FAITHFULLY.

WHAT DO YOU SUGGEST?

TO GO TO THE SHORES OF THE DEAD SEA... AND TO START A COMMUNITY THERE WITH THOSE WHO ARE WILLING TO FOLLOW ME.

*The future Qumran.

ALEXANDRA SALOME, THE WIDOW OF ARISTOBULUS, QUICKLY MADE HER PLANS.

IT IS A WIDOW'S DUTY TO MARRY ONE OF HER DEAD HUSBAND'S BROTHERS.

SO RELEASE MY HUSBAND'S THREE BROTHERS FROM PRISON.

AND ALEXANDRA SALOME MARRIED **ALEXANDER JANNAEUS,** THE ELDEST.

BY MARRYING YOU, I'M MAKING YOU KING...

FOR THAT I'M GRATEFUL TO YOU— AND YOU WON'T BE SORRY...

IT WAS RATHER THOSE OF THE OTHER PARTY, THE PHARISEES*, WHO WERE SORRY...

EVERYTHING HAPPENED SO QUICKLY! WE HAD NO TIME TO DO ANYTHING!

AND HERE WE ARE ONCE AGAIN WITH AN IMPOSTOR, WHO PROCLAIMS HIMSELF KING AND HIGH PRIEST!

*Heirs of the Chasidim. They obeyed the law of Moses in every way.

AT LEAST THE KING WON'T GET WHAT BELONGS TO US!

BURN EVERYTHING!

WEIGHED DOWN BY HIGH TAXES, THE PEASANTS REVOLTED...

WE MUST ORGANIZE A REVOLT! THIS DISGRACE CAN'T CONTINUE!

THE REVOLT WAS CRUSHED WITH TERRIBLE CRUELTY...

I THINK THE PEOPLE REALIZE THAT **ALEXANDER JANNAEUS** IS AFRAID OF NOTHING AND NOBODY!

VERY SOON, MY FRIENDS, OUR NEIGHBOURS ARE GOING TO FIND THAT OUT ALSO!

ALEXANDER JANNAEUS WON SOME BATTLES AND LOST OTHERS.

AH! WHAT A FIGHT!

BUT THE PEOPLE HATED THESE WARS. DURING THE FESTIVAL OF SHELTERS, THE CROWD BOOED THE KING.

YOU'RE NOT FIT TO GO INTO THE TEMPLE!

FALSE PRIEST! FALSE KING!

THESE PEOPLE MAKE ME ANGRY!

IT'S ANOTHER SMACK IN THE FACE BY THE PHARISEES! PACK OF JACKALS! YOU'LL PAY FOR IT!

FROM THAT DAY ON, REBELLION AND REVENGE FOLLOWED EACH OTHER. THOUSANDS LOST THEIR LIVES.

I'VE NEVER SEEN SUCH A HORRIBLE THING! WHILE HE WAS HOLDING A PARTY, JANNAEUS WATCHED 800 JEWS BEING CRUCIFIED. I WON'T STAY ANOTHER DAY IN THIS COUNTRY!

8 000 PEOPLE THOUGHT SO TOO, AND FLED... AFTER THAT THERE WAS NO MORE RIOTING OR OPPOSITION AS LONG AS JANNAEUS WAS KING.

THE GALILEE

SAMARIA

Jerusalem

JUDAEA

MOAB

IDUMAEA

IN HIS REIGN OF 27 YEARS, ALEXANDER JANNAEUS EXTENDED THE HASMONAEAN KINGDOM. HE FORCED EVERYONE IN THE DISTRICTS HE CONQUERED TO BE CIRCUMCISED AND TO OBEY THE JEWISH LAW.

BUT THERE WAS LITTLE UNITY IN THE HASMONAEAN KINGDOM. WHEN JANNAEUS DIED, HIS WIFE, ALEXANDRA SALOME, ACTED IMMEDIATELY.

THIS IS MY PLAN: MY ELDER SON, HYRCANUS, WILL BECOME THE HIGH PRIEST...

...AND THE KING?

NOT FOR THE MOMENT! WE HAVE TO RELY ON THE PHARISEES... FOR THEIR SUPPORT WE CAN DO WITHOUT SOME THINGS...

THE LEADING PHARISEE, SIMON BEN SHETACH, WAS SOON SUMMONED TO THE ROYAL PALACE.

MASTER, AREN'T YOU AFRAID OF A TRAP?

NO! ALEXANDRA IS INTELLIGENT, AND SHE KNOWS THE PEOPLE SIDE WITH US.

SIMEON, IF YOU ACCEPT HYRCANUS AS HIGH PRIEST, I'LL GIVE YOU AND YOUR PEOPLE SEATS IN THE COUNCIL OF ELDERS...

AND... WHO'LL HOLD THE POLITICAL POWER?

I SHALL!

I ACCEPT! THAT WILL SHOW YOU HOW WISE I AM!

THE BOOK OF NUMBERS TELLS US THAT MOSES WAS THE MOST PATIENT MAN ON EARTH...

SO?

WE'VE BEEN RIGHT TO FOLLOW HIS EXAMPLE! TODAY THE SADDUCEES' TIME IS UP!

FOR 9 YEARS, ALEXANDRA SALOME KEPT HER SIDE OF THE BARGAIN, AND INSIDE AND OUTSIDE ITS BORDERS THE COUNTRY WAS AT PEACE. BUT IN 67 BC, AS SOON AS SHE HAD DIED, WHEN HER ELDER SON, HYRCANUS II, BECAME KING...

HYRCANUS, YOUR YOUNGER BROTHER, ARISTOBULUS, HAS RAISED AN ARMY... HE IS MARCHING ON JERUSALEM!

WHEN THE TWO ARMIES MET, SO MANY OF HYRCANUS'S SOLDIERS DESERTED THAT HE HAD TO FLEE JERUSALEM.

HYRCANUS, I COULD HAVE KILLED YOU! SO ACCEPT MY TERMS. LET ME BE PROCLAIMED KING, AND YOU CAN REMAIN THE HIGH PRIEST.

YOUR MAJESTY, I AGREE!

I HAD NO CHOICE... BUT THIS ISN'T THE END OF IT!

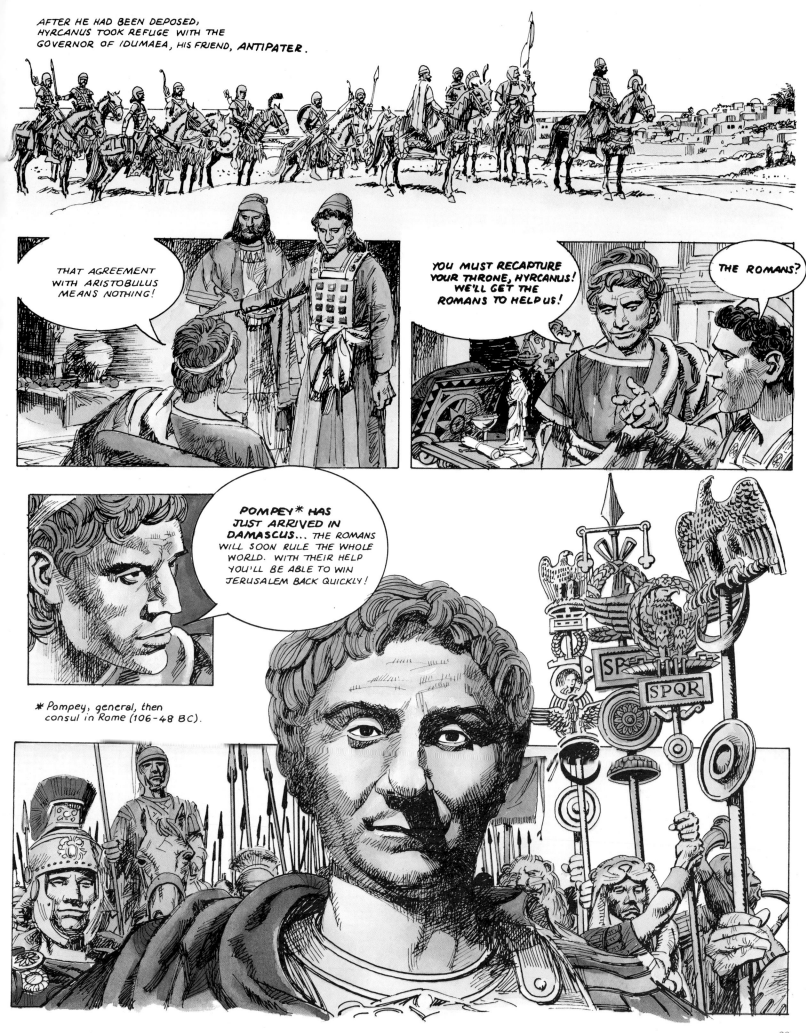

AFTER A SIEGE OF THREE MONTHS, POMPEY ATTACKED IN THE AUTUMN OF 63 BC.

SEIZE ARISTOBULUS! I WANT HIM BROUGHT TO ME ALIVE!

FOLLOWERS OF HYRCANUS SOON OPENED THE GATES TO THE ROMANS.

THEN THERE WAS NO DOUBT HOW THE BATTLE WOULD END, AND ARISTOBULUS HAD TO GIVE IN.

HOWEVER...

MANY THOUSANDS OF STUBBORN PEOPLE HAVE TAKEN REFUGE IN THE TEMPLE.

A DIFFICULT SITUATION!

FILL UP THE DITCH, AND BRING THE TOWERS FORWARD!

LET'S GO AND SEE...

HARD WORK FOR THE ROMAN SOLDIERS...

...MANY MEN DIED THERE.

LOOK OUT!

53 OF OUR MEN HAVE BEEN KILLED.

RIGHT! FROM NOW ON ONLY JEWISH PRISONERS WILL DO THAT JOB!

NOT ONE ROMAN DOWN THERE! WE'RE NOT GOING TO KILL OUR OWN BROTHERS!

THE DITCH WAS FILLED IN. POMPEY HAD THE ASSAULT-TOWERS MOVED FORWARD.

AND WHILE THE FIRST HOLES WERE BEING MADE IN THE WALLS, THE PRIESTS WERE OFFERING THEIR LAST SACRIFICE IN FRONT OF THE MOST HOLY PLACE.

WE PRAISE YOU, LORD, GOD OF THE UNIVERSE, MASTER OF LIFE! WE'RE IN YOUR HANDS...

AT LAST POMPEY REACHED THE TEMPLE COURTYARD.

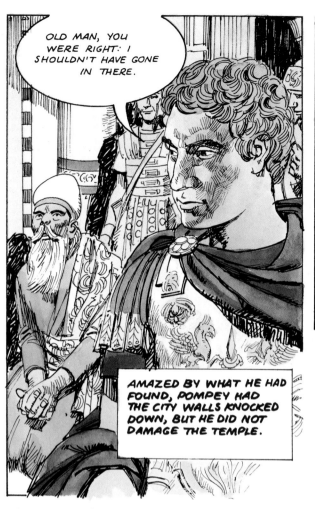

OLD MAN, YOU WERE RIGHT: I SHOULDN'T HAVE GONE IN THERE.

AMAZED BY WHAT HE HAD FOUND, POMPEY HAD THE CITY WALLS KNOCKED DOWN, BUT HE DID NOT DAMAGE THE TEMPLE.

AFTER MAKING HYRCANUS HIGH PRIEST AND GOVERNOR OF JUDAEA AGAIN, POMPEY WENT BACK TO ROME, TAKING ARISTOBULUS AND HIS TWO SONS, ANTIGONUS AND ALEXANDER, WITH HIM.

GET UP! WE'RE GOING ABOARD!

MEANWHILE, IN JERUSALEM...

WELL, HYRCANUS, WASN'T IT A GOOD IDEA TO ASK THE ROMANS FOR HELP?

YES, ANTIPATER, YOU WERE RIGHT. BUT FROM NOW ON WE'LL BE THEIR SUBJECTS!

HYRCANUS, HOW COULD WE HAVE DONE ANYTHING ELSE?

AND FOR 20 YEARS JUDAEA WOULD HAVE ENDLESS TROUBLES...

FAR AWAY FROM ALL THIS, THE MEN OF THE **QUMRAN COMMUNITY** WERE EATING THEIR MEAL, WHILE THEIR LEADER READ TO THEM.

I thank you, Lord: you give light to more than one face.

IN 56 BC, ARISTOBULUS ESCAPED FROM THE ROMAN PRISON, AND TRIED TO STIR UP JUDAEA TO REVOLT. THE ROMANS DEFEATED HIM AND PUT HIM IN PRISON AGAIN.

IN 49 BC, WAR BROKE OUT BETWEEN TWO OF THE THREE ROMAN RULERS, JULIUS CAESAR AND POMPEY. AFTER POMPEY HAD BEEN KILLED IN EGYPT THE NEXT YEAR, JUDAEA SUPPORTED CAESAR.

BECAUSE OF HIS GOOD AND LOYAL SERVICE, CAESAR APPOINTED ANTIPATER THE PROCURATOR OF JUDAEA. HE SOON FOUND GOOD POSITIONS FOR HIS TWO SONS: PHASAEL BECAME GOVERNOR OF JERUSALEM; HEROD GOVERNOR OF THE GALILEE.

HEROD WENT TO ROME, TO ASK MARK ANTONY AND OCTAVIAN FOR HELP. THE ROMAN SENATE PROCLAIMED HEROD KING OF JUDAEA, AND GAVE HIM AN ARMY TO DRIVE OUT THE PARTHIANS.

IN 40 BC, THE PARTHIANS INVADED PALESTINE. WITH THEM WAS ANTIGONUS, THE SECOND SON OF ARISTOBULUS, WHO CLAIMED THE THRONE OF JUDAEA.

AT QUMRAN THE ESSENE COMMUNITY GREW IN NUMBERS, AND WENT ON LIVING FAR AWAY FROM ALL THESE IMPORTANT EVENTS.

A VOICE CRIES:

PREPARE A WAY FOR THE LORD IN THE DESERT, BUILD A ROAD IN THE DRY PLACES FOR OUR GOD...

BUT IN THE SPRING OF 37 BC A MESSENGER ARRIVED AT QUMRAN.

HEROD AND THE ROMANS ARE BESIEGING JERUSALEM!

JERUSALEM! THEN YOU'LL BE SPARED NOTHING!

THESE THINGS HAVE TO HAPPEN! JERUSALEM MUST BE CRUSHED UNDER THE FEET OF THE NATIONS BEFORE THE MESSIAH CAN COME...

...A NEW SIEGE OF JERUSALEM, WHICH WOULD LAST 5 MONTHS.

SOSIUS, THE ROMAN GOVERNOR OF SYRIA, DIRECTED THE ATTACK IN PERSON.

SEE, HEROD? MY TROOPS HOLD THE CITY, AND ANTIGONUS HAS GIVEN HIMSELF UP.

THEN, SOSIUS, PLEASE ACCEPT THIS PRESENT!

SOSIUS, BEFORE YOU GO BACK TO YOUR PROVINCE, SAVE ANTIGONUS FROM HAVING TO WATCH ME BEING CROWNED KING!

SO SOSIUS HAD ANTIGONUS BEHEADED.

BECAUSE HE WAS CLEVER AND CUNNING, HEROD REIGNED FOR 33 YEARS, FROM 37 TO 4 BC.

I HAVE TWO RULES. FIRST, REMAIN FRIENDLY WITH THE ROMANS...

YES, BUT WHICH ROMAN?

THE ONE IN CONTROL, WHOEVER HE MIGHT BE!

SO HEROD WROTE TO OCTAVIAN IMMEDIATELY AFTER HIS VICTORY OVER MARK ANTONY:

I WAS A FAITHFUL FRIEND TO ANTONY. IF YOU TRUST ME, I WILL BE YOUR MOST FAITHFUL FRIEND.

MY SECOND RULE IS TO RELY ON THE PHARISEES, AND DESTROY THE SADDUCEES!

COME ON! MOVE! YOU HAVE TO DIE!

HEROD, ARE YOU PLANNING TO BECOME THE HIGH PRIEST YOURSELF?

THAT WOULD BE STUPID! I'LL CHOOSE SOMEONE WHO SUITS ME...

WHAT A STRANGE MAN KING HEROD IS! ... HE WILL DO ANYTHING!

HE HAD HIS FAVOURITE WIFE, HIS SONS, AND HIS BROTHER-IN-LAW KILLED...

YOUR MAJESTY, THE JOB IS DONE!

PERFECT! FROM NOW ON THERE'S NOT A SHADOW OF A HASMONAEAN LEFT IN THE WORLD!

...AND YOU KNOW WHAT HEROD HAS DECIDED TODAY? HE IS GOING TO SELL HIS GOLDEN CROCKERY, TO BUY CORN FROM EGYPT!